LINES FOR ALL OCCASIONS

Intimidations & Ultimatums

KNOCK KNOCK®
VENICE, CALIFORNIA

Created and published by Knock Knock
Distributed by Who's There, Inc.
Venice, CA 90291
knockknockstuff.com

ISBN: 978-160106113-3
UPC: 825703-50113-1

10 9 8 7 6 5 4 3 2

Contents

"I know a really great taxidermist."

Introduction

We live in an angry, confrontational world. From the cradle to the grave, we're forced to shove, berate, and bully our way through the "age of rage" just to get through the day. If you want to excel in *any* field, however—from dog walking to promotion hunting—you're going to have to polish your tell-offs to a perfect verbal shine. Defending your dominance with a well equipped, challenging quip not only ensures you'll never suffer the shame of sissy-hood again, but will also generally increase your quality of life. As esteemed *Calvin and Hobbes* cartoonist Bill Watterson observed, "A little rudeness and disrespect can elevate a meaningless interaction to a battle of wills and add drama to an otherwise dull day."

Whether you're naturally intimidating or habitually meek, by picking up this book you're well on your way to being—or becoming—an awesomely authoritarian figure. Maintaining a consistent attitude of antagonism can be downright exhausting, however, which is where the lines in *Intimidations and Ultimatums for All Occasions* come in. You'll dominate every confrontation, whether you're the one creating the situation or simply require a response in not-so-kind.

Anyone with a backbone knows that the alleged "golden" rule simply isn't true in post-biblical society. We live in crowded cities filled with loud music, cigarette smoke, and nagging significant others—and *everyone's* pissed off about it. Three out of four people believe that manners have declined in the past thirty years; one in five report workplace bullying; and a full 90 percent of us have experienced an incident of aggressive driving. The good news is that anger is a natural response to the many annoyances that you face. According to a Vanderbilt University study, aggression releases dopamine and is addictive in much the same way that sex, food, and drugs can be (not to mention necessary to defend yourself against the entire angry population). The benefits of fighting back are multiple; researchers at the venerated Mayo Clinic claim that being assertive boosts self-esteem, and as your reputation as a ballbuster increases, so too will others' admiration of you.

Intimidations and Ultimatums is your guidebook to all things intimidating. The threats, demands, and terms and conditions you'll find in these pages will provide the framework for coming out on top—and staying there. Some lines are sheer verbal bludgeons, while others rely on subtle psychological cues that play upon your foe's vulnerabilities. It's up to you to know when to deliver what type of message—hard and mean or sneaky and cruel—and observing your adversaries and loved ones' defense mechanisms will come in handy. Is your opponent openly combative or do they rely

on false displays of confidence?
Are they actually a physical threat?
Are they likely to call you out on
your ultimatum? These are the
types of questions you will have
to ask yourself before delivering
the appropriate intimidation.

In the end, only the strong sur-
vive. With these handy lines in
your arsenal, you're well on your
way to being one of the stron-
gest—and scariest. No more will
you cower meekly in the corner,
greeting others as a doormat to
their success or happiness. The
time has come to take back the
streets. Now, go forth and bully
knowing that you're prepared to
conquer any and every situation.

THE WORKING
WORLD

When they need to know who's boss

PROFESSIONAL LIFE IS OFTEN
fraught with kowtowing and nego-
tiation. Workplaces everywhere
are overrun by a dreaded scourge
of brownnosers and bootlickers,
docile grunts who cultivate obedi-
ence in order to get ahead. Lucky
for you, pushovers are just that—
easy to push over. The meek may
inherit the earth, but they won't sit
in the corner office—you will.

Tip: All in Their Heads

You don't have to be big to bolster your intimidation technique. Put your hands on your hips (an open, unguarded chest implies that you can handle anything flung your way) and subtly set the tone with a well-honed death stare and head nod. Research has shown that glaring at someone increases their heart rate and makes them feel nervous, while listeners are likely to mimic your nod, indicating concession—voluntary or otherwise.

In the politically correct workplace, wimpy attitudes are increasingly the norm; buzzwords such as "compromise" and "mutual respect" filter through the recycled air like so many corporate mandates that have ineffectually come before. You, however, are not fooled by such placating doublespeak. Whether you're already calling the shots or are simply determined to do so, adopting the lines in this chapter as your go-to responses is sure to set you apart from your spiritless coworkers.

As the master of military strategy Sun Tzu wrote in his frequently co-opted *The Art of War*, "It is only one who is thoroughly acquainted with the evils of war that can thoroughly understand the profitable way of carrying it on." Ensuring that you're top dog requires finesse and a willingness to embrace the dark side of intimidation and manipulation, not to mention skillful delivery. Remember, no matter what they fire at you, you have a heavier arsenal—this book—so be fearless and show them what "drill down" really means.

Addressing Underlings

This is not a democracy.

———•◆•———

Plenty of people would *love*
to be in your position.

———•◆•———

I'd really hate to be disappointed.

———•◆•———

You have a lot to learn.

———•◆•———

Can't you do anything right?

———•◆•———

Annual reviews are just
around the corner.

———•◆•———

You've been warned.

———•◆•———

You know the movie about the
scary boss? They based it on me.

Have I made myself clear?

⋅—⋅•⋅—⋅

Put your tail back between
your legs where it belongs.

⋅—⋅•⋅—⋅

And that's an order.

⋅—⋅•⋅—⋅

An app could do what you
do—twice as fast.

⋅—⋅•⋅—⋅

I've got my eye on you.

⋅—⋅•⋅—⋅

Why is this so difficult for
you to understand?

⋅—⋅•⋅—⋅

I *invented* pain points.

⋅—⋅•⋅—⋅

Failure's not an option.

⋅—⋅•⋅—⋅

Know your place, flunky,
know your place.

You're not indispensable.

———•◦•———

Can I see you inside my
office for a minute?

———•◦•———

This is going straight into your file.

———•◦•———

You have to give head to get ahead.

———•◦•———

I've been giving your performance
some thought—and I'm concerned.

———•◦•———

Do you have any idea how many
résumés I receive daily?

———•◦•———

It's simple; you can take
fewer hours or no hours.

———•◦•———

Are you nervous? You should be.

———•◦•———

You'll never work in this town again.

Coffee!

Is this your best work?

Managing Management

Who's coming with me?

The higher you are,
the harder you fall.

I'm the Boss

In the workplace, manipulation is a surefire path
to intimidation. Proving that "reasonable boss"
is an oxymoron, film producer Scott Rudin has
five assistants who are frequently fired (and
rehired and fired) for minor offenses such as
bringing the wrong muffin. In another terrorizing and efficient tactic, Rudin prerecords
demands (e.g., "String cheese NOW!") that are
broadcast with the touch of a button. Yet, being
a Rudin assistant is a highly sought-after job.

My daddy knows people.

I know things.

I'll tweet about this!

Who made you the boss?

We'll unionize.

I'm in high demand.

My nickname was "whistle-blower" at my last job.

I'm calling Human Resources.

How do you sleep at night?

I keep my webcam rolling after hours.

Single. Point. Failure.

———•••———

I figured out how to blind cc.

———•••———

Condoms showed up on
your expense reports.

———•••———

Your skill set is beyond
passé at this point.

———•••———

I know why you're so happy
when you get back from lunch—
and it's not the dim sum.

———•••———

Don't make me go over
your head on this one.

———•••———

I won my last sexual
harassment suit.

———•••———

You left a paper trail.

You're Killing Me

Your boss may take pleasure in your pain, but probably not in your extinction. If your manager is working you to the bone, garner sympathy and fear by dropping hints of *karoshi*, the Japanese term for occupational sudden death. Putting in excessive hours on the job has been linked to cerebral and heart diseases and mental disorders. The first documented case was in 1969, when a healthy twenty-nine-year-old dropped dead at work.

I'll walk.

I'm next year's model.

You're not the boss of me.

I'm starting my own company.

I'll name names.

Double it.

We hate you.

Commanding Coworkers

Welcome to hell.

I have seniority.

You're right—you shouldn't
have told me that.

I know who you *really* are.

They'll assume it was my idea, anyway.

There are pictures from
the holiday party.

Brownnosing has its benefits.

You're not in liberal arts
college anymore, kid.

———

Your doctor's fax just
arrived. Warts, huh?

———

Remember: you friended
me on Facebook.

———

Can you really only do *one*
thing at a time?

———

Why yes, we were talking about you.

———

No one understands why
you work here.

———

You left your résumé in the printer.

———

I have printouts of your photocopied
butt—on office stationery.

You're redundant.

———•———

It's your word against mine.

———•———

I spoke with some of your
former coworkers.

———•———

You're in way over your head.

———•———

Apparently there are stupid questions.

———•———

I'm well known around
the watercooler.

———•———

You put the sub in "subpar."

———•———

I'm onto you.

———•———

Don't make me throw you
under the bus.

One-trick ponies are only
good for a ride.

Everyone knows you slept
your way to the top.

The jig is up.

I will set fire to your cubicle.

I know where you work.

Dominating the Deal

Any questions?

I'm not buying what you're
selling, if you get my drift.

You wouldn't want to shoot
yourself in the foot.

This is going to cost you.

———•◦•———

I heard you the first time, friend.

———•◦•———

Sign up now, or sign up
never; it's your call.

———•◦•———

It's not a question of if—
but when.

Getting Worked Up

Do what you love and love what you do. Turn
power into a paycheck:

- Police officer:
  "Put your hands
  up!"

- Drill sergeant:
  "Drop and give
  me fifty!"

- Interrogator:
  "Where were you
  last night?"

- Wrestler:
  "Piledriver!"

- Monarch:
  "Off with his
  head!"

- Nun:
  "See this ruler?"

- Ninja: N/A; Ninjas
  don't talk.

Good luck with that.

Do you want to be ahead of
the curve or behind?

We can do this the easy
way or the hard way.

Great deals like this don't last long.

Just sign on the dotted line.

There are people who would *love*
to be riding this inside track.

There's no need to get emotional.

You're going to have to trust us on this.

You don't want to miss out on
this amazing opportunity.

You obviously don't know
what you're talking about.

———•◦•———

And here I had you pegged as
a leader, not a follower.

———•◦•———

I'm the good cop here; you don't want
me to bring in the bad cop, do you?

———•◦•———

Show me the money!

ROMANCE

When you want to be on top

FACE IT: LOVE AND SEX MAKE YOU vulnerable. Physically, emotionally, and/or metaphorically, no matter how you slice it, you're naked. While experts suggest that successfully navigating the landscape of love requires compromise, these so-called authorities are wrong. The only way to ensure you get your romantic needs met is to take control. After all, the experts also

Tip: That's a Deal-Breaker

Relationships are a deal—and you're allowed to break deals, and hearts, if things aren't going your way (or at least threaten to). Begin all requests, with "If you love me, you'll ..." Use this tactic no matter how trivial or profound your wish may be, whether you want the dog fed or to procreate. For additional ammo, end your plea with "...or I'll leave." Your paramour is sure to take the emotional bait and you'll be sure to get your way.

agree that self-confidence lures people to you, a key component in attracting future dates to dominate.

The course of true love may never run smooth, but remaining unruffled during entanglements is only possible if you're the one wearing the pants—and they're not. According to lifestyle website PopSugar.com, 3I percent of read-ers said they would give a spouse an ultimatum if provoked. Once you put yourself in this group and use the lines here, you'll be on the winning side of any encounter, from discouraging losers at the outset to maintaining dominance when committed to getting frisky.

Unfortunately, there may come a time when an affair will end. Don't despair; prevailing through post-romance is covered, too, and with well-timed deployment you'll be in control even if there isn't a prenup.

Remember: whether dating, committed, or divorcing, the line between tactical manipulation and abuse must be respected. Manipulating others is fun and helps you get what you want. Abuse is just wrong and makes you a terrible, terrible person.

Deterring Deadbeats

My boyfriend's bigger than you.

My last girlfriend was a model.

I carry mace.

I'm a professional.

Currently I'm filming a reality
series about being a single
parent with seven children.

Have you ever heard of
vagina dentata?

I would eat you alive.

I have heels that are bigger
than what you're packing.

Buy me a drink—or else.

I'm out of your league.

My dad's a cop.

My mom's a cougar.

I like to think of myself as a strong, independent woman.

I have really high standards.

I'm huge.

You can't afford me.

You don't want what I have.

I have crabs.

Controlling Commitment

It's me or fantasy football.

It's me or the macramé club.

There *are* other fish in the sea.

I have a certain image to live up to. You're not living up to it.

Get a job or get lost.

I'm thinking about leaving.

Nail biting is a deal-breaker.

Chronic masturbation is a deal-breaker.

I don't see a ring on my finger.

Make an honest woman of
me or I'll start lying.

———•◦•———

Do *you* feel sexually fulfilled?

———•◦•———

I have options.

———•◦•———

I told you from the beginning I
wasn't looking for anything serious.

You Go, Girl

In 1993, Lorena Bobbitt made good on a
common wifely threat: she cut off more than
50 percent of her philandering, abusive hus-
band's penis while he slept. She then tossed it
into a field, where it was later found and reat-
tached. When questioned by police, Bobbitt
commented, "He always have orgasm and he
doesn't wait for me to have orgasm. He's self-
ish. I don't think it's fair." The jury found her
not guilty due to temporary insanity.

We need to talk.

———•———

We need to stop talking.

Manipulating Marriage

Marriage is a contract.

———•———

My mother could come stay
with us for a while.

———•———

If you don't bring home dinner,
then we just won't eat.

———•———

Who else would put up
with your crap?

———•———

I'm dissatisfied.

———•———

I'll flush when you're in
the shower.

Don't test me.

———•—•———

How would you know if I
forgot to take the pill?

———•—•———

No dishes, no sex.

———•—•———

No dusting, no blowjob.

———•—•———

My clock is ticking.

———•—•———

I'll be bringing this up in therapy.

———•—•———

I watch you when you sleep.

———•—•———

This is how it starts.

———•—•———

The worst is yet to come.

———•—•———

This is how it ends.

Asking for It

The threat of being flogged, whipped, or having your genitals "manipulated" seems like it would be unappealing to most. Dominatrices, however, get paid—two hundred dollars per session, on average—to fulfill such submissive fantasies. According to the Kinsey Institute, 5 to 10 percent of Americans participate in this type of sex play, known as BDSM (bondage, discipline, dominance, submission, sadism, and masochism). Welcome to the dungeon.

I own you.

'Til death do us part.

Strong-Arming Sex

Was that it?

I'll tell all your friends
how small you are.

The handcuffs are in the top drawer.

———•—•———

I was faking it.

———•—•———

If you really loved me, you'd
have a threesome.

———•—•———

No glove, no love.

———•—•———

I've never had an orgasm.

———•—•———

I filmed us.

———•—•———

Get on your knees.

———•—•———

Don't make me sit on your face!

———•—•———

I have the warts.

———•—•———

Size does matter.

You can't compete
with the rabbit.

———•◦•———

My ex was an extraordinary lover.

———•◦•———

I used to be a man.

———•◦•———

I used to be woman.

———•◦•———

I have needs.

———•◦•———

Harder! Faster!

———•◦•———

No kissing, no coitus.

———•◦•———

I'm a big deal in the
S&M community.

———•◦•———

I'm a third-level, chakra-attuned
tantric all-star—shazam!

There's a pill for that.

———•◦•———

You're such a clitourist.

———•◦•———

Choke me.

Bullying Through a Breakup

You signed the prenup.

———•◦•———

You'll be nothing without me.

———•◦•———

Go ahead, break up with me: your mom will be devastated, all our friends will take my side, the stress will affect your job and you'll be fired, and eventually you'll die a sad, lonely death.

———•◦•———

I know all your passwords.

———•◦•———

Revenge is sweet.

My lawyers will crush you.

———•———

I'll get the house.

———•———

I'll get the cars.

———•———

I'll get the dog.

———•———

Sleeping with your best
friend isn't beneath me.

———•———

The kids are going to hate
you for this.

———•———

You'll be fat and penniless
when I'm through with you.

———•———

Hell hath no fury.

———•———

Don't underestimate me.

I can drag this out for *years*.

———————

You can run, but you can't hide.

———————

I'll walk with *more* than half.

———————

I'll set fire to your bed.

———————

Get out!

The Dotted Line of Love

Don't be blinded by love; it's always good to have a plan B. Know the law—and make it—in order to maximize your relationship leverage. A prenup provides adequate intimidation to keep your lover in check. Only 5 to 10 percent of couples actually sign one, but formalizing the details is worth the fuss. When Steven Spielberg divorced Amy Irving without the precautionary paperwork, for example, she walked away with a cool $100 million.

FRIENDS
AND FAMILY

When you know best

WHEN YOU THINK "FAMILY," NO
doubt the next thing that comes to
mind is "power struggle." From the
antagonistic child-parent dynamic
to sibling rivalries to master-pet
codependency, the very foundation
of our personal networks is built
on the necessity of subjugation,
manipulation, and intimidation.
And the same is true for friendships
(there's a reason why "unfriend"

Cautionary Tales

Fairy tales have long spooked children into submission with the most intimidating scepter of all: consequences. The classics provide explicit fates for naughty little boys and girls—just think of Goldilocks, Hansel and Gretel, and Little Red Riding Hood. Who wouldn't be cowed by the moral of such stories: confronted by angry, feral carnivores, held captive and fattened by a blemish-covered hag, or swallowed whole by a depraved, cross-dressing wolf?

was chosen to be the *New Oxford American Dictionary's* 2009 word of the year). Whether you do it directly or subtly, being the head of the family, clique, or pack always requires a show of command.

All too often, cultural references to family are mired in the misconception that we're bonded with warm, fuzzy feelings of love and mutual admiration. You, of course, know this isn't true. Ever since Cain slew Abel, the primary characteristics of most familial relationships have been dysfunctions, which, lucky for you, are easily abused. Let your clan members know who the head honcho *really* is by mastering the lines found in this chapter. Their foibles and shortcomings will never get in your way again.

Contentious friends and family, however, may feel entitled to retaliate—especially siblings. They know you best, and they're well acquainted with your Achilles' heel, whatever that may be. Use your close knowledge of their flaws and quirks to your advantage and target *them*. Exploit their insecurities and you'll soon be the most powerful presence in the playground, living room, or barbecue.

Overpowering the Progeny

An A- is the gateway to failure.

———•———

Do as I say, not as I do.

———•———

Why would anyone buy the cow if
they can get the milk for free?

———•———

There *are* such things as monsters.

———•———

Do you want to live with grandma?

———•———

Time out.

———•———

Just you wait until your
father gets home.

———•———

I brought you into this world—
I can take you out of it.

Some species of animals
eat their young.

————•◦•————

It's my job to make your
life miserable.

————•◦•————

You'll have your own
kids someday.

————•◦•————

Your face will freeze that way if
you don't eat your vegetables.

————•◦•————

You're going to end up
just like your sister.

————•◦•————

My house, my rules.

————•◦•————

We aren't *obligated* to pay for
your college tuition.

————•◦•————

Because I said so.

Make me proud.

I'm not afraid to homeschool you.

Santa Claus doesn't bring
presents to naughty children.

Why don't you just walk home?

You should be grateful.

You have until I count to three.
One . . .

Power Tripping the Parents

Do you want me to call
Child Services, mother?

My friends' parents would
understand.

I'm not your baby anymore.

———•·•———

You're an embarrassment.

———•·•———

Soon enough I'll be eighteen.

———•·•———

I want to live with mom.

———•·•———

I want to live with dad.

Certain Doom

Threatening our own demise is a common, effective ultimatum. "I'll just die if I don't
_____," is sure to induce a response from even the most stubborn of adversaries. Deliver cautiously, though; there could be unwanted repercussions. For example, take the young protagonist of Shel Silverstein's poem, "Little Abigail and the Beautiful Pony." In the end, Abigail "DID die— / All because of a pony / That her parents wouldn't buy."

You're ruining my life.

One day, I'll put you in a home.

What's the difference between
a diploma and a GED?

I want to be an artist
when I grow up.

You'll never see your grandkids.

My diary is chock-full of material
for my tell-all memoir.

When I go to college, I'll do drugs,
have sex with strangers, and
never call home.

I'll tell mom about the
personal trainer.

I'll tell dad about the plumber.

One word: emancipation.

I'll cultivate mystery bruises.

You're the one that has to
pay for my therapy.

I'll get a face tattoo.

No dad, I am smarter than you.

You'll live to regret this.

Get a life.

I'll never leave home.

I'll hate you forever.

Tip: Because We Care

Sometimes your ultimatum alone will not be enough to sway troubled friends and family. In these cases, it's time to call in the troops and organize an intervention. Your target may lie, beg, cry, deny, and even try to leave—don't let them get away with it. Conclude the confrontation with "if you refuse the help we're offering you today . . . " and provide hefty consequences if they don't comply. En masse, your message will be stronger *and* more threatening.

Sibling Supremacy

I'm telling.

You'll never be the favorite.

They gave *me* power of attorney.

I have baby pictures.

I have teenage pictures.

———•—•———

I'll out you.

———•—•———

You were an accident.

———•—•———

You were adopted.

———•—•———

I'm not giving you any more
money and I never want to
hear from you again.

———•—•———

Don't you ever get tired of
being the black sheep?

———•—•———

Grow up.

———•—•———

I know the *real* you.

———•—•———

I know you played doctor
with our cousin.

Wedgie!

I read your diary.

You're turning into mom.

Grandma loves me best.

You're going to wish you
were never born.

I'll torch Barbie's Malibu
dream house.

I'll rip off Optimus Prime's
arms and legs.

I'll always be younger than you.

I'll always be more successful
than you.

I win.

You lose.

Forceful Friendships

Don't you want to be popular?

I know all your secrets.

You'll never live this down.

Do you want my
honest opinion?

I knew you when you were goth.

I'll unfriend you.

Give me your keys or I'm
calling the police.

You're wearing *that*?

———•••———

I'll post ugly pictures of you.

———•••———

My therapist thinks you're toxic.

———•••———

I'll take you down with me.

———•••———

I dare you.

———•••———

Stop copying me.

———•••———

If you give me a discount, I'll hang
out with you this weekend.

———•••———

I'll remember that.

———•••———

Want a friend? Get a dog.

———•••———

I have a new best friend.

I'll tell everyone you're bulimic.

I know what you did last summer.

Establishing Primacy with Pets

It's really easy to kill a fish.

You're the first to go during a famine.

The People Whisperer

Cesar Millan's award-winning series, *Dog Whisperer*, has inspired a generation of pet owners to behave as "calm-assertive pack leaders" in order to ensure submission. Techniques include establishing "ownership of territory" and making the animals work—and wait—for rewards (such as the right to eat). Being top dog is also appealing to parents. *Whisperer* fans, and some therapists, have begun promoting his methods for child rearing. Tssst.

You're just a dog.

Neutering's not illegal for
animals—in fact, it's encouraged.

I'll give you the fleas.

Listen, ferret.

I'll put you in my purse.

You'll never live up to Lassie.

You'd look just *charming*
with a poodle cut.

Don't make me feed you
to the snake, rodent.

Rabbit's a delicacy.

You've already used up eight
of your lives.

———•·•———

Bath time.

———•·•———

Crate.

———•·•———

Muzzle.

———•·•———

No!

DAILY LIFE

When the world requires your two cents

WE LIVE IN A CONFRONTATIONAL age. You can barely leave the house without encountering incompetents wielding their limited sources of so-called authority with total disregard for superiors in presence and ability—you. Wading through daily life practically *requires* your domination in order to ensure that your basic needs are met: getting your steak cooked the perfect shade

Tip: Reputational Capital

Make your threats more convincing by garnering a reputation for following through on them. According to experts at the Harvard Business School, you only need to make good on one or two threats to gain what is called "reputational capital," which proves that you're serious and lends credibility to all subsequent intimidations, no matter how fake, empty, or outlandish. As a result, your (weaker) opponent will more than likely back down.

of pink, guaranteeing unlimited time on the treadmill, and clearing the lanes for a speedier commute. The only way to get by—and get ahead—is to match the prevalent culture of antagonism with your own bluster.

Whether you're getting a checkup, taking the dog out for fresh air, or have found yourself behind bars,

deliver the lines in this chapter
with steely-eyed reserve to empha-
size the malevolence of your intent.
The world is full of insecure
types who will try to counter your
aggression with their own mis-
guided threats, masking weaknesses
with bombast. Don't be fooled;
simply double your efforts and cultivate a befitting bad attitude, and
not just the garden-variety, passive-
aggressive bumper sticker sort.

Finally, if face-to-face doesn't do
it for you, take your power to the
Internet. Sites like Yelp.com can
turn frustrations into command-
ing threats of boycott and the loss
of business. While apologists may
advocate a turn-the-other-cheek
approach, *you* know the only thing
that this will accomplish is another
slap—so post and demand your
way through every day.

Restaurant

I have contacts at the
Health Department.

You call this gazpacho?

Let me speak with your manager.

I'll Yelp about this!

How do you *know* I'm not a
food critic?

The customer is always right.

Rat!

Doctor's Office

I'm highly contagious.

A high percentage of patients
win medical malpractice suits if
the case goes all the way to court.

------•◦•------

Give me the drugs and
no one gets hurt.

------•◦•------

I'll splatter on the pee cup.

------•◦•------

Why don't *you* bend over?

------•◦•------

The AMA would be very
interested in your "alternative"
treatment methods.

------•◦•------

I heard about your little prick.

Therapist's Office

How do *you* feel?

------•◦•------

I feel like acting out.

Do I make you nervous?

———•———

Analyze *that*.

———•———

It takes one to know one.

———•———

Are those your children
in that picture?

———•———

I'll kill myself.

———•———

My inner child murders
small animals.

———•———

I love you.

School

Locker raid!

———•———

Report to the principal's office.

This is going on your
permanent record.

———•———

You can't, in fact, do anything
you set your mind to.

———•———

Use your words.

———•———

We're going to have to
call your parents.

E-timidation

No longer limited to the schoolyard or the
parking lot, intimidation is now just a click
away. Whether you choose to cyber-bully or
cyber-stalk, terrorizing others has never been
easier. The web's anonymity—not to mention
all the personal dirt you can possibly dig up—
makes it an attractive alternative to being
ruthless in person. Just remember, though;
don't dish it out if you can't take it. The flow
of information goes both ways, after all.

Spit out your gum and
get a brain.

Fail.

Car

Idiot!

Dumbass!

Jerkoff!

Moron!

Jackass!

Douchebag!

Asshole!

Ship

Hit the decks!

———•·•———

Your coxswain will never
be the same again when I
get through with you.

———•·•———

Avast—don't make
me use my bimmy!

———•·•———

We're a long way
from land.

———•·•———

We'll mutiny.

———•·•———

Man overboard!

———•·•———

Walk the plank, privateer.

———•·•———

Give up your booty!

The Not-So-Mighty Warriors

With names like the Raiders and the Giants, some sports teams strike fear in the hearts of their opponents. Others fall flat:

- Anaheim Ducks
- Chicago Cubs
- Los Angeles Angels
- Miami Dolphins
- New Jersey Nets
- Orlando Magic
- Pittsburgh Penguins
- Toronto Blue Jays
- Toronto Maple Leafs
- Utah Jazz
- UC Santa Cruz Banana Slugs

Sporting Event

Let's settle this score.

———

Your balls are deflated.

———

I hope for your sake you're wearing a cup.

———

I'll see you at halftime.

Choke!

Is that all you've got?

Eat my dust.

Bang bang choo-choo train
Wind me up and I'll do my thang,
I know karate, I know kung fu,
You mess with me, I'll mess with *you*!

Gym

Run! Run! Run!

I could bench-press you.

I've seen you naked.

You should really get some
new workout clothes.

Your endorphins can't
save you now.

———•———

My biceps are hella huge.

———•———

Feel *this* burn.

Dog Park

I know a really great taxidermist.

———•———

You call that a dog?

———•———

If you don't shut that
thing up, I will.

———•———

Bitch.

———•———

Sic 'em.

———•———

Watch out—he's a humper.

Bite me.

———•••———

I bite too.

Places of Worship

I will crucify you.

———•••———

Say your prayers.

———•••———

Two words: hairy palms.

———•••———

I will rain vengeance
down upon thee.

———•••———

Get on your knees.

———•••———

Yahweh sees all.

———•••———

I can make your life
a living hell.

An eye for an eye.

———•———

Satan's my homie.

———•———

The end is nigh.

Jail

Don't drop the soap.

———•———

I'll narc.

———•———

See you in the yard.

———•———

I've got friends on
the outside.

———•———

What do I have to lose?

———•———

I'll strike a deal with
your prosecutor.

We'll riot.

———•◦•———

I need a new bitch.

———•◦•———

I'll shank you.

———•◦•———

Imagine what solitary *does* to a person.

———•◦•———

Gimme your cornbread.

Go to Hell

A mainstay of believers everywhere, hell provides the ultimate threat. Descriptions of the underworld vary greatly—from ancient Greek's melancholy Hades to Dante's divine, convoluted inferno to Jean-Paul Sartre's "other people"—but eternal damnation remains singularly daunting. Employ this time-honored theme with standards such as "Burn in," "See you in," and "I'll send you straight to," and let others know exactly where you wish they'd go.

CHARACTERISTICS

When you're better than them

THE FACT THAT THE SELF-HELP industry is booming—books espousing positive psychobabble generate at least $1 billion annually—indicates that people are full of insecurities to exploit. From looks to empty coffers to a personal sense of total failure and/or general asininity, everyone's ashamed of something. You, however, are equipped with the proper

Not Another Pretty Face

They're clearly intimidated by your beauty—
no, really, they are. Numerous researchers
have proven that beauty is actually power.
According to studies, attractive people
make more money, are judged more posi-
tively, and are even given more space on side-
walks. If you're not a natural beauty, however,
work on showing off your good taste and self-
confidence. Good looks, even the kind you
have to work for, can make knees go weak.

tools (the lines in this book)—
not to mention your undeniable
supremacy—to guarantee victory
when waging psychological war.

Most are already the weaker foe,
having acceded to now-standard
politically correct mores. Our über-
polite age ensures that a well-honed
and below-the-belt attack will be
a surprise. Once you've debilitated

them emotionally, they'll question their very self-worth, making them vulnerable to the whims of your threats ever after.

Having depleted another's self-esteem, kudos is in order—you're doing them a favor. The resulting unfavorable comparison to your dominance can only spell a new-found contentment: understanding their rightful place in the pecking order will free them from the baggage of self-delusion when contrasted with your clear superiority.

If you're not the smartest, best looking, youngest, richest, or morally purest—it doesn't matter. Intimidating others is about who they think you are, which is better than them, and not some abstract idea of perfection. Bluster until they bow to your dominance.

Intimidating with Intelligence

I'm a MENSA member.

———•◦•———

You didn't know the answer?

———•◦•———

That's an *interesting* idea.

———•◦•———

I graduated summa cum laude.

———•◦•———

I challenge you to a game
of Scrabble.

———•◦•———

My thesis focused on the
architectural speciation of
synthetic particles and flawed
neurochemical interactions.

———•◦•———

Vous ne parlez pas français?

———•◦•———

I *am* a rocket scientist.

I read—a lot.

———•—•———

I've actually finished *Remembrance of Things Past*—by Proust.

———•—•———

Will you be attending the party for my Pulitzer?

———•—•———

It's not my fault you can't follow sesquipedalian phraseology.

———•—•———

I'll slow down so you can understand.

———•—•———

Am I understood?

———•—•———

Prove it.

———•—•———

Where did you matriculate?

———•—•———

I'm smarter than you.

Attacking Appearances

Don't you think you're
trying a little too hard?

———•———

I wouldn't say you're a
natural beauty.

———•———

You call that an outfit?

———•———

Who are you wearing?

———•———

I don't even wear makeup.

———•———

My metabolism works
out *for* me.

———•———

You can't buy bone structure.

———•———

Your girlfriend thinks
I'm hot.

Your boyfriend wants to do me.

———◆———

My high school voted me
best looking.

———◆———

You look good—for your age.

———◆———

Are you *sure* you want to
super size that?

Looking the Part

Disney villains have played a role in what
generations of children—and the adults
they grow into—find fearful. The bad guys'
most common characteristics are thin faces,
pointy eyebrows, long incisors, a turned-down
mouth, and an approximate age of fifty-five.
Although a majority of the intimidators are
men, according to the American Film Institute,
the most frightening animated villain of all
time is *Snow White*'s Queen.

You have such a pretty face.

———•◦•———

Superlatives don't do me justice.

———•◦•———

Me—ow.

———•◦•———

These are real.

———•◦•———

It's nice to see they put some
style in the larger sizes.

———•◦•———

I'm too sexy for this book.

———•◦•———

They call me McDreamy.

———•◦•———

I'm hotter than you.

Assailing Based on Age

I know where you keep
your dentures.

I'll pull the plug.

———•———

Isn't it your bedtime?

———•———

It's a good thing you're wearing
your adult diapers today.

———•———

Toupées are incredibly
flammable.

———•———

Give me the prunes and
no one gets hurt.

———•———

What does irrelevancy feel like?

———•———

I'll make it so you fall—
and can't get up.

———•———

Cougars kill.

———•———

Brittle bones are the easiest to break.

Tip: You Don't Scare Me

Don't let anyone turn the tables and direct a threat your way. If provoked, be calm, defend your personal space (especially behind you), and don't isolate—always have witnesses. Remember, psychological manipulation is intended to make you appear unstable or paranoid. An unflappable demeanor is a necessity not only for rebuttals, but also for reversing dominancy so you can return to your position as top intimidator.

Do you have a problem
with that, *ma'am*?

It's a good thing you won't
hear me coming.

You think you have arthritis *now*?

At your age, everyone will
assume it was natural causes.

Your days are numbered.

———•—•———

I'll report you to the DMV.

———•—•———

Can't you afford botox?

———•—•———

You would think you'd have
your life together by now.

———•—•———

I'm younger than you.

Dictating with Dollars

Everyone has a price.

———•—•———

Name your price.

———•—•———

Where do you summer?

———•—•———

My assistants can
take care of that.

I live in Manhattan.

———•—•———

I don't *have* to work.

———•—•———

Who's your daddy?

———•—•———

There's low class, and then
there's no class.

———•—•———

Turns out, money can
buy happiness.

———•—•———

We know *you* weren't a legacy.

———•—•———

Have you ever made love
on a pile of money?

———•—•———

Please refer to me as "Count."

———•—•———

Have your people talk to
my people.

Lets discuss this at my villa.

Where *did* you buy those pants?

You can't buy blue blood.

My island is beautiful this
time of year.

I make more money than you.

I make more money than God.

Cutting Down Others' Character

I have the truth on my
side—and pictures.

I'll show you what "bitch" means.

I would never do what you did.

Your hostility makes you
an easy target.

———•◦•———

I spend all my free time volunteering
to help those who are less fortunate
than I am—what do you do?

———•◦•———

What goes around comes around.

———•◦•———

No one misses a bad seed.

———•◦•———

Everyone loves me.

———•◦•———

I'll kill you with kindness.

———•◦•———

What happens in Vegas doesn't
always stay in Vegas.

———•◦•———

How do you live with yourself?

———•◦•———

Karma's a bitch.

I drive a Prius.

————•·•————

I recycle—
and compost.

————•·•————

My children are multicultural
and attend *public* school.

————•·•————

I'm better than you.

Passively Aggressive

You don't have to be openly hostile to
intimidate people—being overbearing in other
ways works, too. Put the "right" back in self-
righteous by using a patronizing tone, brag-
ging about your bleeding heart, and providing
commentary on the kind of person "who would
do such a thing." By honing these holier-than-
thou benchmarks of mothers and do-gooders
alike, you're sure to evoke others' easily manipulated feelings of guilt and inadequacy.

FAMOUS FIGHTING WORDS

When you need to bring in the big guns

HISTORY IS CHOCK-FULL OF triumphant tyrants, dictators, professional assholes, and those that just play one in the movies. These are all worthy sources to refer to when developing your persona as a threatening individual, because after all, who better to consult than the likes of politicians, monsters, and Mr. T? They succeeded so thoroughly at intimidation that

Talk to the Hand

To really hammer home your message, use your hands. But be sure to consider your location. Many friendly gestures to be avoided stateside can be employed abroad. For instance, the "okay" sign means "asshole" in Brazil and Germany, and in parts of West Africa, South America, and the entire Middle East "thumbs-up" implies "shove it." No matter where you are, however, pointing (or wagging) your finger at your target is always a threat.

they became famous (or infamous) for it. Follow their lead and you too will reach the top of your game, be it professional, recreational, or downright criminal.

While the previous chapters took you on a guided tour of lines to repeat verbatim in particular circumstances, general inspiration is now your guide. Since by this point you will have an even greater appreciation for the talent it takes to deliver an effective intimidating line or ultimatum, you'll be even more impressed by the finesse found in these examples.

If this book has done its job well—not that anyone in their right mind would dare to disagree—your head should now be filled with menacing admonishments and a desire to go forth and bully. If you want to take your newfound interest in intimidation to the next level, consider brushing up on the works of some of those featured in this chapter, whether by watching the films or reading their respective biographies. Before you know it, you too could be quoted in the great pantheon of people who know how to get what they want.

Strong-Arming Sports

"I want to eat his children."
—Mike Tyson

"We are in the business of kicking
butt and business is very, very
good." —Charles Barkley

"Dead meat!" —Mr. T,
as Clubber Lang in *Rocky III*

"We're gonna yank 'em and tear 'em and
rrrrip 'em. We're gonna take 'em and roll
'em around and rip 'em up to pieces.
And then we're gonna slaughter 'em!"
—Sid Caesar, as Coach Calhoun in *Grease*

"If you've got a Corvette that runs
into a brick wall, you know what's
gonna happen. [Kobe's] a corvette.
I'm a brick wall. So you know what's
gonna happen." —Shaquille O'Neal

"I'll beat him so bad he'll need a shoehorn to put his hat on." —Muhammad Ali

❖

"I'm gonna open his hole like this. Please excuse my French. I'm gonna make him suffer. I'm gonna make his mother wish she never had him—make him into dog meat." —Robert De Niro, as Jake La Motta in *Raging Bull*

❖

"If you aren't fired with enthusiasm, you'll be fired with enthusiasm." —Vince Lombardi

❖

"When I retire, I'll get Ricky Hatton to wash my clothes and cut my lawn and buckle my shoes. Ricky Hatton ain't nothing but a fat man. I'm going to punch him in his beer belly. He ain't good enough to be my sparring partner." —"Pretty Boy" Floyd Mayweather

❖

"Get him a body bag, yeah!" —Rob Garrison, as Tommy in *The Karate Kid*

"You better watch it, Dr. Death. I'm pretty damn fast for a Caucasian."
—Robin Williams, as Jack Dundee in *The Best of Times*

"The price is wrong, bitch!"
—Adam Sandler, as Happy Gilmore in *Happy Gilmore*

Business Bulldozers

"I invented 'It's a good thing' before you were even born."
—Martha Stewart

"The buck stops with the guy who signs the checks."
—Rupert Murdoch

"Now listen up, Mr. Pink. There's two ways you can go on this job: my way or the highway. Now what's it gonna be, Mr. Pink?" —Lawrence Tierney, as Joe Cabot in *Reservoir Dogs*

"The details of your incompetence do not interest me." —Meryl Streep, as Miranda Priestly in *The Devil Wears Prada*

"I could crush him like an ant. But it would be too easy. No, revenge is a dish best served cold. I'll bide my time until . . . Oh, what the hell. I'll just crush him like an ant." —Mr. Burns on *The Simpsons*, created by Matt Groening

Bring It On

Long-standing team rivalries have resulted in classic—and creative—trash-talk traditions. Many schools provide underground "cheer sheets," offering choreographed taunts of the opposition's shortcomings. At the private Northwestern University, for instance, an intimidating crowd of nearly 50,000 chants of "state school, state school" accompanied by jingling car keys—implying that the public competition will soon be parking their cars.

"If any of my competitors were drowning, I'd stick a hose in their mouth." —Ray Kroc

———•◦•———

"The day is quickly coming when every knee will bow down to a silicon fist, and you will all beg your binary gods for mercy." —Bill Gates

———•◦•———

"When I get ahold of the son of a bitch who leaked this, I'm gonna tear his eyeballs out." —Michael Douglas, as Gordon Gekko in *Wall Street*

———•◦•———

"I have a very assertive way. It's wake up, move your ass, or piss off home." —Gordon Ramsay

———•◦•———

"I'm an ice queen, I'm the Sun King, I'm an alien fleeing from District 9 and I'm a dominatrix. So I reckon that makes me a lukewarm royalty with a whip from outer space." —Anna Wintour

"Put. That coffee. Down. Coffee's for closers only." —Alec Baldwin, as Blake in *Glengarry Glen Ross*

"You get back in here and finish what you started. Do you hear me?" —Demi Moore, as Meredith Johnson in *Disclosure*

"You're fired." —Donald Trump

Imposing Politicos

"We don't negotiate with terrorists." —U.S. Vice President Dick Cheney

---

"If you want a picture of the future, imagine a boot stamping on a human face—forever." —O'Brien in *Nineteen Eighty-Four*, by George Orwell

---

"Why don't you shut up?" —King Juan Carlos I of Spain

Turn It Off

Music can set the mood for impending doom—think *Jaws*. It can also be the doom itself, as employed by the U.S. military. Torturous tunes condoned by the Bush Administration to torment and intimidate at Guantánamo Bay (and beyond) include a surprisingly diverse range. Bruce Springsteen's "Born in the U.S.A.," Christina Aguilera's "Dirrty," the theme song from *Barney & Friends*, and several AC/DC hits have all been blasted to make detainees squeal.

"We are not amused." —Queen Victoria

"It's a good day to die." —Crazy Horse

"We will pursue the terrorists everywhere . . . if we catch them on the toilet, we will wipe them out in the outhouse." —Russian President Vladimir Putin

"Hail to the chief, if you don't, I'll have to kill you. I am the chief, so you better watch your step, you bastards."
—James Garner, as Former President Matt Douglas in *My Fellow Americans*

"The time will come for the men responsible for this to answer for their behavior, but not today."
—U.S. Congressman Tom Delay

"We're both sticking to our guns. The difference is, mine are loaded." —Gary Oldman, as Shelly Runyon in *The Contender*

"If I see you, I'm going to punch you in the face." —Colombian President Álvaro Uribe Vélez

---

"Good and decent people must be protected and persuaded by gentle means, but the rabble must be led by terror." —Napoleon Bonaparte

"Katie Graham's gonna get her tit caught in a big fat wringer if that's published." —Nixon Administration Attorney General, John N. Mitchell

———•———

"Nuke 'em. Let's nuke the bastards." —Bill Pullman, as President Thomas Whitmore in *Independence Day*

———•———

"Piss off, old man!" —Polish President Lech Kaczynski

———•———

"I will make you shorter by the head." —Queen Elizabeth I

Commandeering Criminals

"I bite." —Jeffrey Dahmer

———•———

"I'm going to make him an offer he can't refuse." —Marlon Brando, as Don Vito Corleone in *The Godfather*

"We serial killers are your sons, we are
your husbands, we are everywhere. And
there will be more of your children
dead tomorrow." —Ted Bundy

———•—•———

"Your suffering will be legendary,
even in hell!" —Doug Bradley, as
Pinhead in *Hellbound: Hellraiser II*

———•—•———

"I'll be back." —Arnold Schwarzenegger,
as the Terminator in *The Terminator*

———•—•———

"You can get more with a nice
word and a gun than you can with
a nice word." —Al Capone

———•—•———

"Say hello to my little friend!"
—Al Pacino, as Tony Montana in *Scarface*

———•—•———

"Maybe if I stick your head through that
window over there you'll get unconfused."
—Joe Pesci, as Nicky Santoro in *Casino*

"Let's get 'em boys!" —Richard Connaught,
as Billy Boy in *A Clockwork Orange*

———•———

"People thought me bad before, but if
ever I should get free, I'll let them know
what bad means." —Billy the Kid

———•———

"Tell me something, my friend.
You ever dance with the
devil in the pale moonlight?"
—Jack Nicholson, as Joker in *Batman*

———•———

"From the world of darkness I did
loose demons and devils in the
power of scorpions to torment."
—Charles Manson

———•———

"You talkin' to me? You talkin' to
me? You talkin' to me? Then, who
the hell else are you talkin' to? You
talkin' to me? Well, I'm the only one
here. Who . . . do you think you're
talkin' to?" —Robert De Niro,
as Travis Bickle in *Taxi Driver*

"I wipe my ass with your feelings."
—James Gandolfini, as Tony
Soprano on *The Sopranos*

Basic Bullies

"If I wasn't feeling so ladylike right
now, I'd bitch slap you all the
way to the coffee machine."
—Kathy Kinney, as Mimi Bobeck
on *The Drew Carey Show*

Tip: What's in a Name?

Give yourself a threatening nickname and intimidate with a simple introduction. First, pick a subject that you excel at—so your new alias has credibility. Then, select a topic-specific sharp tool, predatory animal, or other menacing element. Finally, be definitive and add "The." Good at cooking? Become "The Slicer." Enjoy surfing? Consider "The Shark Tooth." Even innocuous hobbies such as knitting can make for powerful pseudonyms, i.e., "The Needle."

"These five fingers . . . individually,
they're nothing, but when I curl
them together like this into a single
unit, they form a weapon that is
terrible to behold!" —Lucy in *Peanuts*,
created by Charles M. Schulz

———•◦•———

"You've got to ask yourself one question:
do I feel lucky? Well, do ya punk?"
—Clint Eastwood, as Police Inspector
Harry Callahan in *Dirty Harry*

———•◦•———

"Im'a get medieval on your ass."
—Ving Rhames, as Marsellus
Wallace in *Pulp Fiction*

———•◦•———

"Respect my authoritah!"
—Eric Cartman on *South Park*, created
by Trey Parker and Matt Stone

———•◦•———

"You blow it tonight, girl, and it's keggers
with kids all next year." —Kim Walker,
as Heather Chandler in *Heathers*

"You don't scare me, freak. Underneath all that hair, you're still a dork, Scott. I've handled your kind before. Your mama used to steal chickens out of the backyard until I blew her head off with a shotgun." —Mark Arnold, as Mick McAllister in *Teen Wolf*

———•————

"So, why don't you make like a tree and get outta here?" —Thomas F. Wilson, as Biff Tannen in *Back to the Future*

———•————

"What is your major malfunction, numbnuts? Didn't Mommy and Daddy show you enough attention when you were a child?" —R. Lee Ermey, as Gunnery Sergeant Hartman in *Full Metal Jacket*

———•————

"Say Uncle! Say it!" —Zack Ward, as Scut Farkus in *A Christmas Story*

"My biceps are hella huge."